Original title:
Rising from Ruins

Copyright © 2024 Swan Charm
All rights reserved.

Author: Liisi Lendorav
ISBN HARDBACK: 978-9916-79-267-4
ISBN PAPERBACK: 978-9916-79-268-1
ISBN EBOOK: 978-9916-79-269-8

Hope's Hands in Halos of Light

In humble hearts, the dawn does rise,
With gentle whispers from the skies.
In faith we reach, in love we stand,
Hope's warm embrace, a guiding hand.

Through trials dark, through storms we tread,
The light of truth shall be our thread.
In every tear, a prayer takes flight,
Hope's hands in halos, shining bright.

With every soul that walks beside,
In unity, our hearts abide.
For in each heartbeat, sacred grace,
We find our strength, we find our place.

The Pilgrim's Path through the Ashes

Amidst the ruins where shadows rest,
The pilgrim walks, with heart possessed.
Through ashes cold, and whispered cries,
He seeks the truth, where spirit lies.

With each small step on broken ground,
In faith he walks, with hope profound.
Embers fade, yet light remains,
The soul's journey, through joys and pains.

In every footstep, echoes stay,
Voices from night, to greet the day.
The ashes tell of what has been,
Yet rise in grace, for life comes in.

Reunited in Reverence

From distant shores, our spirits meet,
In sacred bond, we find our seat.
With open hearts and hands in prayer,
We gather close, for love does care.

In every laugh, in every sigh,
In quiet moments, we draw nigh.
With reverence deep, our voices rise,
Together now, beneath the skies.

Through time and trials, we have grown,
In every seed of faith we've sown.
Reunited, let our spirits sing,
In harmony, our praises ring.

A Covenant in the Chaos

In chaos bright, where shadows play,
A covenant forms, to light the way.
In woven paths of grace we tread,
We seek the truth, our spirits fed.

Amidst the storms, the tempest's roar,
Our hearts unite, forevermore.
With every breath, a promise made,
In love we trust, and fears will fade.

For in the chaos, grace expands,
A sacred pact, with open hands.
Together bound, we stand as one,
In the chaos, we are never done.

The Sacred Seed of Tomorrow

In gardens deep where faith does bloom,
The sacred seed breaks through the gloom.
With gentle hands we sow our plight,
In hope's embrace, we find the light.

From hallowed ground, new life will rise,
Where trials fade and joy complies.
Each tear we shed, a drop of grace,
In turning winds, we find our place.

Let every heart feel love's warm glow,
As branches reach, our spirits grow.
In unity, we stand, we pray,
For brighter dawns, a brand new day.

The roots of love entwine our souls,
In every breath, the music rolls.
With whispered prayers, we tend the seed,
In faith we flourish, love our need.

Awake, arise, let visions soar,
For in our dreams, we seek for more.
The sacred moments, pure and rare,
Will guide us with a tender care.

Reflection in the Ruins

In shadows cast by ancient stone,
We seek the truth in whispers grown.
The echoes of the past resound,
In every crack, a story found.

Among the debris, hope still glows,
In every fracture, beauty shows.
With humble hearts, we bow and see,
The lessons etched in history.

Each fallen wall, a tale to tell,
Of love and loss, of heaven and hell.
In silence deep, the soul awakes,
A sacred space, where faith remakes.

The dust of ages, rich and wise,
In every eye, a prayerful rise.
In ruins, we find grace anew,
A pathway forged, a life so true.

Together we weave through the decay,
Finding the light that guides our way.
In reflection, let our spirits soar,
For from the ruins, we are reborn.

The Reverberation of Resurrection

In stillness deep, the heart does beat,
A whisper calls, a sacred greet.
From depths of night, new dawn will break,
In every soul, the chance to wake.

The echo of a promise made,
In darkest hours, our fears will fade.
With hope reborn, we rise anew,
As wings unfold, the sky is blue.

From ashes lost, we find our flame,
In heavy chains, we call His name.
The reverberation pierces night,
With each embrace, the world feels right.

In mountains high and valleys low,
A melody we came to know.
With hearts aflame and spirits free,
Resurrection sings in harmony.

Awake, arise, for life is near,
In every breath, the love we hear.
In faith we stand, our hearts aligned,
The sacred rhythm, pure and kind.

A Song of Solace from the Shattered

In brokenness, a melody,
From shattered dreams, we come to see.
With trembling hands, we lift our voice,
In sorrow's grasp, we make a choice.

Each note a tear, each word a prayer,
In darkest times, we feel Him there.
With every chord, the heart lays bare,
A song of solace fills the air.

Amidst the pain, we find the strength,
To rise again, to go the length.
For in the cracks, the light will gleam,
A tapestry woven from our dream.

With gentle winds, our spirits soar,
In love's embrace, we seek for more.
In unity, we stand as one,
A symphony begun, yet never done.

From every wound, a seed will sprout,
A testament beyond all doubt.
Through shattered lives, the hope will gleam,
In melodies of love, we dream.

Redemption in the Ruins

In shattered places, hope will rise,
A light that breaks through heavy skies.
With every tear, a future blooms,
From ashes, love dispels the glooms.

The hearts once lost, now find their way,
In shadows cast by yesterday.
With every prayer, a whisper grown,
In ruins deep, we're not alone.

Through trials faced, our spirits mend,
A journey starts where sorrow ends.
With faith as strong as ancient stone,
We build anew, we find our home.

The path of grace, though rough and bare,
Leads us to joy beyond despair.
In brokenness, a thread of gold,
The story of redemption told.

Let every moment pulse with light,
In darkest hours, we seek the bright.
Together, hand in hand we stand,
In ruins found, we heal our Land.

Wings Born of the Wreckage

From wreckage wild, new life will soar,
In fragile forms, we seek for more.
With tender hope, we rise from dust,
In faith's embrace, we find our trust.

Each battered branch bears fruit anew,
In darkest nights, we search the blue.
With wings of grace, we learn to glide,
Through storms that rage, our hearts abide.

The light that warms, a gentle hand,
In broken dreams, we make our stand.
From trials faced, our spirit frees,
In every loss, new victories.

Though shadows cloak the path we tread,
A flame ignites where fear has fled.
With courage born of shattered past,
In wreckage, we are free at last.

Emerging strong, we take the flight,
On wings of love, we touch the light.
In harmony, our voices blend,
From wreckage born, our souls ascend.

The Sacred Path of Restoration

In quiet whispers, grace unfolds,
A path of light where warmth beholds.
With every step, the heart beats strong,
In sacred trust, we all belong.

Through trials deep, our spirits weave,
In brokenness, we learn to believe.
With gentle hands, we craft anew,
The sacred path that calls us through.

In loss, we find a deeper gain,
Through rain and sun, we bear the pain.
With eyes of faith, we see the seeds,
Of love's great harvest, all our deeds.

Each moment bears a chance to heal,
In restoration, we can feel.
With open hearts, we seek the way,
The sacred love that lights our day.

Together, souls in unity,
Walk steadfast through each mystery.
On sacred ground, we rise and shine,
In restoration, the heart divine.

Whispers of the Redeemed

In gentle sighs, the lost are found,
A symphony of grace resounds.
With every breath, the past released,\nIn whispered prayers, we find our peace.

The voices rise, a chorus sweet,
In moments shared, our hearts repeat.
From shadows cast, we spark the flame,
In silence soft, we call His name.

The stories told, of battles fought,
In every tear, a lesson sought.
With every soul, a journey shared,
In love's embrace, we are prepared.

For in the night, the stars will gleam,
In darkest hours, we still can dream.
With faith held close, our spirits dance,
In whispers soft, we find our chance.

To walk the path the faithful paved,
In light of truth, all hearts are saved.
As whispers fade, a truth redeemed,
In love's pure light, we are esteemed.

Steps of Faith through Desolation

In shadows deep, we tread with care,
Each step whispers a sacred prayer.
Through barren lands, our hearts remain,
In faith we rise, despite the pain.

The path unknown, yet light will guide,
In desolation, hope abides.
With every trial, our spirits soar,
In trust, we see a brighter shore.

Though storms may roar, we stand as one,
Through darkest nights, we sense the Sun.
With hands held high and voices raised,
We march in faith, forever praised.

The journey long, but strength is found,
In unity, we break the ground.
As dawn breaks forth, our dreams ignite,
In steps of faith, we find our light.

So here we stand, in truth ablaze,
With every heartbeat, we give praise.
In desolation, we find grace,
United, we will seek His face.

The Measure of Lost Innocence

In tender years, we learned to dream,
With eyes so bright, life's sweetest gleam.
Yet shadows creep, the world unfolds,
And innocence fades, like whispers told.

The measure lost, in fleeting time,
Where purity fades, like unsung rhyme.
Yet through the sorrow, we learn to stand,
In every loss, a guiding hand.

The journey's pain shapes hearts anew,
For in the loss, we gain what's true.
With open hearts, we seek to mend,
What once was broken, we can defend.

In wisdom's embrace, we rise again,
From ashes born, we conquer pain.
Each scar a mark of battles fought,
In every lesson, hope is wrought.

So as we walk through darkened days,
We trust in love's unending ways.
For lost innocence may fade from view,
But in our souls, His light breaks through.

Serene Sanctum of the Shattered

In shattered hearts, a silent plea,
To find the peace that sets us free.
In fragility, we seek His grace,
In every crack, His light we trace.

Quiet moments, where fears dissolve,
In stillness, we find souls evolve.
Though pieces lie in disarray,
In gentle hands, we find our way.

The sacred space invites us near,
To feel the strength amidst our fear.
With faith restored, we breathe anew,
In shattered forms, His love breaks through.

The journey bends, yet does not break,
In every loss, a chance to wake.
Through brokenness, we learn to see,
The beauty found in unity.

So let us gather, broken yet bold,
In our sanctum, stories unfold.
For in the shattered, peace we find,
A healing balm for every mind.

A Testament to Renewal

From ashes rise, a phoenix strong,
In every end, we find a song.
With hopeful hearts, we seek the dawn,
In every trial, a newness born.

The seasons shift, as nature knows,
In death, rebirth, the spirit grows.
Through rocky paths, we learn to tread,
With every tear, new blooms are fed.

In the silence, whispers call,
A testament to rise from fall.
With every breath, we forge ahead,
In moments lived, our fears are shed.

So let the past no longer bind,
For in our hearts, the truth we find.
Each step a note in life's great score,
A testament to love, and more.

As hands join hands, we face the light,
In unity, we find our might.
With faith ablaze, we journey on,
In renewal's grace, we greet the dawn.

The Light Beyond the Collapse

In shadows deep where silence grows,
A flicker shines, when darkness flows.
With every heart that seeks to find,
The promise of a light, divine.

Amidst the ruins of our plight,
Faith whispers softly through the night.
A beacon calls, a guiding grace,
To heal the wounds, and time erase.

When hope seems lost and spirits fade,
A truth anew begins to cascade.
From ashes born, we rise once more,
To taste the joy that we adore.

In every tear, a seed we sow,
In every prayer, the courage to grow.
Through trials fierce, the soul will thrive,
Embraced by love, we're truly alive.

The light emerges, soft and pure,
It leads us home, steadfast and sure.
In unity, our voices blend,
To seek the dawn, where shadows end.

Rebirth in Divine Embrace

In quiet hush of dawn's first light,
A gentle whisper breaks the night.
With every breath, renewal flows,
In sacred arms, our spirit grows.

From fallen leaves, new life will spring,
The promise held in everything.
We learn to trust the path ahead,
In faith, we rise, where angels tread.

Each moment gifts a chance to rise,
To glimpse the truth behind the skies.
The past will fade, like morning mist,
In divine love, we shall persist.

In trials faced, we find our grace,
With open hearts, we seek His face.
Through every storm, through every tear,
In love's embrace, we conquer fear.

Rebirth be ours, in sacred light,
Awakened souls, ignited bright.
As flowers bloom and seasons change,
In faith we dance, our hearts rearranged.

Miracles on the Brink of Oblivion

In desperate times, where hope seems frail,
A miracle whispers in the veil.
In darkest nights, the stars align,
To show the way, a spark divine.

With heavy hearts and burdens borne,
We seek the grace where love is worn.
A gentle hand upon the soul,
To guide the lost, to make us whole.

From chaos springs a tender peace,
In moments brief, our fears release.
When whispers fade and echoes die,
A miracle, we can't deny.

Beside the edge of all we know,
A leap of faith begins to grow.
With open hearts, we soar above,
Together bound, in endless love.

In every heartbeat, magic lies,
In every tear, a new sunrise.
When faced with shadows deep and stark,
The light of grace ignites the spark.

A Psalm for the Fallen

In memory's breath, we softly tread,
For those we've lost, for words unsaid.
With aching hearts, we raise a song,
In honor true, where they belong.

For every tear that graced their face,
We gather here, to seek His grace.
With folded hands and spirits bare,
We find the strength within our care.

In whispered prayers, their light remains,
Through sorrow's depths, through endless pains.
In every shadow, love will flow,
For those who've wandered, we still know.

In every moment, their lives inspire,
The flame of hope, a burning fire.
We carry forth their cherished dreams,
In heart's embrace, love reigns supreme.

As dawn awakens, so shall we,
In unity, our souls fly free.
For fallen ones, our hearts will sing,
In sacred bond, our spirits cling.

Celestial Kiss of the New Dawn

In the stillness, light breaks free,
A whisper from eternity.
Golden rays, a tender touch,
Transforming shadows, oh so much.

Heaven's brush paints the sky,
Inviting hearts to rise up high.
Each morning holds a sacred grace,
An echo of the divine embrace.

With every breath, hope is reborn,
In the glow of a new dawn.
Embrace the day, let spirits soar,
Find solace in the light we adore.

As petals open to the sun,
Unified, we become one.
The world awakens, renewed, clear,
In the warmth, we shed our fear.

Celestial kisses, softly sent,
Fill our hearts with pure intent.
Through darkness, we have come to see,
The dawn unveils our destiny.

Harvesting Hope from Grief

From sorrow's soil, our roots run deep,
In the silence, secrets keep.
Tears like rain, nurtured seed,
In the shade, new life will lead.

With every loss, a lesson learned,
In the ashes, passions burned.
The strength we find amid the pain,
Is the light that breaks the chain.

Gather the fragments, one by one,
Transform the night, pursue the sun.
In every heartache, hope will bloom,
A sacred promise, dispel the gloom.

With open arms, we tend the field,
To grief's embrace, our hearts shall yield.
Each bitter day, the cycle spins,
For in our loss, true life begins.

Harvesting dreams from what has passed,
In love's remembrance, we stand steadfast.
Together we rise, hand in hand,
Faithful souls in a healing land.

The Blessing of the Broken Path

On twisted roads, where shadows creep,
The heart learns lessons, oft' so steep.
In fractured light, we find our way,
A testament to brighter days.

Each stumble leads to deeper grace,
As we journey through sacred space.
With each misstep, we rise anew,
From brokenness, our souls breakthrough.

The blessing found in paths unknown,
Is in the seeds of faith we've sown.
Courage born from trials faced,
In every loss, love embraced.

We walk with purpose, slow and sure,
The broken path, a sacred cure.
With every scar, a story told,
In humility, our hearts behold.

So let us cherish each winding turn,
For in the struggle, we shall learn.
The light that guides, forever near,
In every step, we shed our fear.

The Serene Shrine of Regrowth

In quiet gardens, life returns,
Where patience dwells, and wisdom yearns.
Among the ashes, love will thrive,
A sacred refuge, we come alive.

Roots entwined in tender soil,
In each challenge, our spirits toil.
From gentle storms, new shoots appear,
The promise held in every tear.

A sanctuary, calm and bright,
Where dreams take flight in sacred night.
In every leaf, a tale unfolds,
Embracing warmth in arms so bold.

The trees they whisper, softly sway,
Guiding souls along the way.
With faith, we gather what we need,
In the shrine of grace, we heed.

So let us gather 'neath the sky,
In tender moments, we rely.
From darkened days to radiant glow,
In our hearts, the seeds will grow.

The Elixir of Endurance

In the silence of prayer, strength will arise,
A balm for the weary, a light in the skies.
Faith weaves through the trials, steadfast and true,
A potion of courage, from hearts ever new.

Through shadows and fears, His grace does abide,
In moments of doubt, let the spirit be tied.
With every struggle, there's wisdom in pain,
Each drop of endurance, a beautiful gain.

Seek solace in hymns, let your spirit take flight,
In valleys of darkness, emerge into light.
The elixir of hope flows gently and clear,
A river of mercy, washing away fear.

The Anointment of the Anxious

When anxiety whispers, and courage seems frail,
The anointment of peace, a spiritual gale.
With hands raised in prayer, the heart learns to breathe,
In whispers of comfort, the soul finds reprieve.

Each drop of His love, a balm for the night,
In times of uncertainty, embrace the true light.
With faith as a shield, the burdens grow small,
In the dance of His mercy, we rise, we stand tall.

Let the weary find rest in this sacred embrace,
As hope fills the heart, and fear leaves no trace.
The anointment of calm, a gift from above,
In the stillness of trust, we discover His love.

Tribute to the Tenacious

Ode to the steadfast, who walk through the fire,
With spirits unbroken, they rise ever higher.
Through storms and through trials, their faith stays alive,
In the heart of the struggle, the tenacious strive.

Their hands shall not falter, their will shall not bend,
For each step they take, a purpose to mend.
With eyes on the promise, the dawn breaks anew,
In the tapestry woven, the tenacious pursue.

In unity forged, they whisper a song,
A testament written where dreams do belong.
With courage in spirit, they face what is near,
A tribute to strength that conquers all fear.

Hope's Harvest from the Hollow

In the depths of the hollow, where shadows may dwell,
Emerges a harvest, a story to tell.
From sorrow's rich soil, hope blooms in the night,
A testament woven with threads of pure light.

Each tear that is sown, turns to gold in the morn,
As faith's gentle whisper brings forth a new dawn.
What once felt like loss, now bears fruit to share,
Hope's harvest, a treasure, found in deep prayer.

Embrace all the trials that life has bestowed,
For within every struggle, a blessing will goad.
In echoes of glory, the spirit takes flight,
From the hollow of heart, rises hope, pure and bright.

Virtues Born in the Void

In silence deep, where nothing dwells,
A whisper stirs, the heart compels.
From void's embrace, the light breaks free,
Virtues arise, in humility.

Through shadows cast, grace finds its way,
In the darkest night, hope finds its day.
The spirit's quest, a sacred fight,
To find the path, through endless night.

With faith as anchor, love as guide,
We journey forth, we do not hide.
In trials faced, we seek the true,
Shaping the soul, in every hue.

From ashes rise, a phoenix plumed,
In every heart, the fire resumed.
In unity strong, we stand so tall,
Each virtue born, to heed the call.

In the void's depth, the spirit sings,
Of ancient truths, and timeless things.
As we embrace, the vast unknown,
In every breath, a virtue grown.

Lamentations Turned to Lullabies

In quiet shadows, tears do fall,
Each drop a story, an unspoken call.
From sorrow's depth, a song will rise,
Lamentations turned to lullabies.

When burdens weigh, our spirits bend,
In pain we find, a faithful friend.
Through every hurt, a beauty shines,
In broken hearts, the light entwines.

With every sigh, the soul is freed,
In whispered prayers, we plant the seed.
Through trials faced, we learn to trust,
In love's embrace, our hearts adjust.

As night draws near, and peace descends,
The rhythm flows, the heart transcends.
In every lull, a hope ignites,
From lament's depth, we grasp the lights.

Through darkest hours, we find our way,
The dawn will break, it's here to stay.
With open hearts, we shall abide,
In lullabies where faith resides.

The Gospel of Renewal

In every dawn, a promise shines,
A testament to love's designs.
With every breath, the spirit grows,
The gospel flows, like rivers' throes.

Through trials faced, the soul is taught,
In struggles won, redemption sought.
From ashes rise, a bloom anew,
In every heartbeat, grace is true.

The sacred text, a whisper soft,
In gentle winds, our spirits loft.
With faith as guide, we walk the path,
Embracing joy, forsaking wrath.

With hands outstretched, in service be,
A gospel shared, for all to see.
In kindness poured, the world awakes,
Through love we find, the peace it makes.

From shadows cast, to light's embrace,
In every soul, we find our place.
The gospel calls, to hearts aligned,
In renewal's grace, the truth defined.

Broken Yet Blessed

In fragments lie, our stories told,
In every crack, a heart of gold.
Though broken road may lead us far,
In depths of darkness, shines the star.

With scarred hands raised, we give our all,
In every stumble, we shall stand tall.
For every wound, a lesson learned,
In every tear, a beacon turned.

With humble hearts, we seek the pure,
In faith's embrace, the soul's allure.
Though shattered dreams may haunt the night,
In the brokenness, we find the light.

In simple acts, of love and grace,
The blessings flow, in every place.
For in the flaws, we understand,
Together bound, we take a stand.

Though broken yet, we carry on,
In the dance of life, the spirit's song.
For blessings grow, where hearts connect,
In every breath, we find respect.

The Covenant of Resilience

In shadows cast by trials deep,
A promise sworn, we do not weep.
With faith as strong as mountain stone,
In every heart, His love is sown.

Through storms that rage, through darkest night,
We find our peace in holy light.
In unity, we rise anew,
The covenant, both strong and true.

Though doubts may whisper, fears may call,
We stand together, never fall.
For every pain, a lesson learned,
In every flame, a heart that burned.

As petals fall, yet blooms return,
In every loss, we seek to learn.
With open hands, we bless the day,
In Love's embrace, we find our way.

Resilience flows like rivers wide,
In holy trust, we will abide.
Through trials faced, our spirits soar,
In sacred bonds, forevermore.

Echoes of Redemption

In quiet whispers, souls arise,
A search for grace 'neath endless skies.
Each heartbeat sings a song of hope,
In faith, we learn to rise and cope.

The shadows dance, but light remains,
In tears of sorrow, love contains.
With each misstep, redemption near,
In brokenness, His voice we hear.

From ashes born, we find our peace,
In every trial, we seek release.
Forgiveness flows like rivers true,
In every heart, He makes us new.

Echoes of love resound so clear,
No fear can bind, nor doubt appear.
Together, we shall stand and fight,
For every soul is draped in light.

The path may twist, but hearts align,
In unity, our spirits shine.
With every step, we walk in grace,
In echoes sweet, we find our place.

The Holy Flourish

In gardens lush, His blessings bloom,
With every breath, dispelling gloom.
In sunlight's kiss and morning's dew,
The holy flourish, ever true.

Seeds of compassion, deeply sown,
In fertile hearts, His love has grown.
Through seasons change, we stand our ground,
In sacred grace, new life is found.

With open hands, we share our gifts,
In kindness, love forever lifts.
A tapestry of joy divine,
In every heart, His light will shine.

Through summer's warmth and autumn's chill,
The holy flourish bends our will.
In every moment, we rejoice,
In living faith, we find our voice.

For every trial, a blossom brings,
In gratitude, our spirit sings.
Within His garden, souls entwine,
In holy flourish, love will shine.

Veils of Distress Unraveled

When burdens weigh and shadows fall,
In quiet prayer, we heed the call.
With heavy hearts, we seek the light,
In veils of distress, we find our fight.

With grace, the chains begin to break,
In every sorrow, love's awake.
Through trials faced, our faith prevails,
In unity, the spirit sails.

The whispers of despair may fade,
With every breath, a hope remade.
As dawn breaks forth, our vision clear,
In open hearts, we cast our fear.

Through tears of anguish, beauty grows,
In sacred silence, love bestows.
Each veil undone, a promise seen,
In every soul, the light will glean.

For every cross, a victory song,
In darkened night, we still belong.
With faith unshaken, we arise,
In veils of love, our spirits rise.

Beneath the Shattered Halo

In the glow of sacred light,
We wander in the still of night,
Searching for the lost divine,
Beneath the shattered halo's shine.

Whispers of grace that fade away,
Hope clings faintly to the day,
Yet hearts in turmoil seek the way,
To find a promise in the fray.

With hands held high and heads bowed low,
We trace the paths where spirits go,
In every tear a prayer is sown,
A testament to love once known.

The stars align, a fleeting chance,
For souls to rise and learn to dance,
In sacred spaces, we reclaim,
The light within that bears the name.

Though shadows linger, darkness weaves,
We find our strength in bending knees,
Beneath the halo, broken yet bright,
We are reborn within the light.

Out of the Shadows of Despair

In the valley of grief we tread,
Where whispers of hope seem long dead,
Yet from the ashes, faith can grow,
In the dark, the spirit's glow.

The suffering teaches the heart to yearn,
With each trial, the soul can learn,
To rise above what brings us low,
A flicker of grace in each sorrow.

In the quiet, where doubts entwine,
We seek the face of the divine,
A love unbroken, vast and deep,
Awakening dreams that we still keep.

Embracing pain as part of the plan,
With every wound, we understand,
That joy awaits beyond the tears,
In the light, dispelling fears.

So from despair, we choose to rise,
With hearts ablaze and open eyes,
Out of the shadows, strong we stand,
United in faith, hand in hand.

The Holy Rebirth

In the silence of the dawn,
A whisper calls as life moves on,
From ashes cold, a spirit soars,
Emerging free from ancient shores.

Each heartbeat marks the sacred time,
Of love renewed, of faith sublime,
The cycle turns as stars align,
In the holy dance, the soul will shine.

With every tear, a seed is sown,
In pain, the depths of grace are known,
Through trials faced, the heart finds peace,
In rebirth's arms, our fears release.

From winter's chill to springtime's bloom,
Transcending shadows, banishing gloom,
We rise anew with purpose clear,
In holy light, our path appears.

Embrace the journey, every part,
For in this sacred work of art,
The holy rebirth whispers still,
To seek, to heal, to love, to will.

Echoes of the Forgotten

In the stillness of the night,
We hear the echoes take their flight,
Whispers from the past resound,
In spaces lost, new hopes are found.

The stories fade, yet hearts remain,
Marked by love, and filled with pain,
Like shadows cast by ancient dreams,
In silence, gather strength that gleams.

Through time's embrace, we tread the line,
Between what's lost and what can shine,
For every heart, a tale endured,
In the forgotten, souls reassured.

The chorus calls from distant shores,
In every heart, the spirit roars,
Reminding us we're never alone,
In echoes bold, we find our home.

So let us listen, let us learn,
From stories told and bridges burned,
For in the echoes of the night,
The forgotten rise to greet the light.

The Beacon Among the Broken

In shadows dim, where hope is lost,
A light shines bright, no matter the cost.
The weary souls find rest anew,
In faith and love, we see it through.

With broken hearts, we seek the way,
In prayers whispered at close of day.
The beacon glows, a guiding hand,
To lead us from this troubled land.

For every tear that falls like rain,
A promise lives to heal the pain.
Among the broken, grace abounds,
In every heart, redemption sounds.

Together we rise, from ashes come,
A symphony of hope, we hum.
In every struggle, we shall find,
The strength to love, to stay aligned.

So let this light shine ever clear,
To chase away the darkest fear.
Among the broken, we stand tall,
For love can conquer, conquering all.

An Ode to the Overcomers

Oh, valiant hearts, who dared to dream,
Through trials fierce, you found the beam.
In storms that raged and shadows cast,
You stood your ground, you held steadfast.

With every wound, you bore the pain,
You learned to dance in springtime rain.
For in the struggle, strength was found,
The echoes of your fight resound.

Each step a testament to grace,
In darkest valleys, you embraced.
The light within you brightly glows,
A spirit fierce, as courage grows.

To those who've risen from the fall,
Your voices lifted, break the thrall.
An ode we sing, in praise, not fear,
The overcomers stand right here.

So wear your scars like badges bright,
For every battle yields the light.
Together, onward, we shall roam,
In love, united, we call home.

Shores of Serenity after the Storm

When tempests roar and fears take flight,
We seek the calm, the soft dim light.
On shores of peace, our hearts find rest,
A refuge found, in faith, we're blessed.

The waves may crash, the winds may howl,
Yet, through the chaos, we'll not prowl.
For every storm shall pass away,
And bring us dawn, a brighter day.

With every tear, a lesson learned,
In trials fierce, our spirits earned.
Together we rise, hand in hand,
As hope's soft whispers fill the land.

Oh, shores of grace that gently call,
To every weary, lost, and small.
In unity, we stand as one,
As hearts embrace, the battle's won.

So let the storms rage, let them strive,
In faith and love, we come alive.
For on these shores, forevermore,
We find our peace, our heaven's door.

Wisdom Woven in Wreckage

In brokenness, a new path forms,
From scattered dreams, the spirit warms.
For through the wreckage, light will shine,
A tapestry of love divine.

Each crack and crevice tells a tale,
Of strength in struggle, hearts prevail.
With wisdom birthed from trials faced,
In every shard, a soul embraced.

From ashes rise, the phoenix sings,
A dance of hope, on fragile wings.
With every scar, a story shared,
In unity, we're always bared.

So gather 'round this sacred space,
With open hearts, we find our grace.
For wisdom woven in the night,
Guides us through darkness, toward the light.

In wreckage lies our sweetest gift,
A bond of love that cannot shift.
Together, strong, we journey forth,
In every heart, we find our worth.

The Sacred Mosaic of Renewal

In shadows cast by weary days,
A spark ignites, a gentle blaze.
Through trials faced and burdens borne,
New life emerges, hope reborn.

Each piece of heart, a story told,
In shattered paths, the soul turned bold.
The sacred art of healing flows,
In unity, the spirit grows.

The hands of love, they stitch the seams,
Creating, mending, weaving dreams.
In every fragment, truth does dwell,
A tapestry where voices swell.

From fragments lost, a picture bright,
Illuminates the darkest night.
Together, we rise and shall proclaim,
Renewed in faith, we call His name.

Eternal grace, the guiding light,
In whispered winds, we find our flight.
With open hearts, we seek to find,
The sacred mosaic, intertwined.

Graces from the Splinters

In every wound, a lesson deep,
A path of growth for souls to keep.
From splinters harsh, new graces form,
In troubled seas, the hearts stay warm.

Each jagged piece, a sacred sign,
That brokenness may still align.
In reverence, we learn to see,
The beauty found in misery.

The hands that heal are often worn,
Through trials faced, the spirit's born.
In shared despair, the light we chase,
A bond created through His grace.

With gentle words, we lift the veil,
To find the strength where others fail.
In life's debris, we choose to glean,
The lessons etched in what has been.

So let us walk on splintered roads,
Embracing all that love bestows.
In every tear, a sacred thread,
From splinters come the graces spread.

The Reverent Ascendance

Upon the hills where silence dwells,
The echoes of the spirit swells.
In every breath, a prayer ascends,
To heights where love and grace transcends.

With every step, a journey blessed,
We seek the truth, our souls at rest.
In reverence, we rise above,
Embracing peace, the gift of love.

Through trials faced, we find our way,
With faith as guide, we strive, we pray.
In soaring hearts, the promise grows,
A light that through our spirit glows.

The paths we walk, though worn and steep,
In whispered hopes, our secrets keep.
Through every storm, we stand our ground,
In sacred bonds, our strength is found.

To heavens bright, we lift our voice,
In unity, we make our choice.
With reverent hearts, we ascend the skies,
To meet the dawn with open eyes.

Uplifted by Grace

In fields of mercy, spirits blossom,
With gentle hands, we seek the awesome.
Each moment cherished, a gift adored,
Uplifted by grace, our hearts restored.

Through valleys low and mountains grand,
We walk together, hand in hand.
In every struggle, love ignites,
Uplifting souls, dispelling nights.

The whispers soft, like morning dew,
Remind us of our journey true.
In every tear, a seed is sown,
A testament to love we've known.

With faith as compass, we will stand,
In sacred moments, hearts expand.
Embracing light that guides our way,
Uplifted by grace—day by day.

So let us soar on wings of trust,
In every heart, the sacred thrust.
With grace as our eternal guide,
In love's embrace, we shall abide.

Threads of Grace in the Tattered

In the weave of sorrow, a thread pulls tight,
Soft whispers of mercy, bring forth the light.
Each frayed edge tells a story profound,
In the hands of the Maker, lost souls are found.

Beneath the weight of burdens we wear,
Grace flows like rivers, healing despair.
The tattered remains are stitched with care,
Hope shines through shadows, a balm to share.

With faith as our fabric, we walk each day,
In the tapestry woven, we find our way.
The colors of kindness, vibrant and bold,
Embrace every heart, their warmth unfolds.

As threads intertwine, a sacred design,
Our lives mirrored gently, in love's sacred line.
Each knot holds a promise, a prayer in the night,
In the dance of our souls, we gather the light.

Together we rise, as a quilt stitched true,
In the arms of the Spirit, we are born anew.
The threads of our stories, though tattered and worn,
Are woven in grace, for hope is reborn.

The Reclamation of the Soul

In the echoing silence, a heart calls aloud,
Yearning for freedom, beneath pain's shroud.
Dust trails of memory, lost in the past,
Reclaiming the spirit, unbound, at last.

With each step of faith, we gather our might,
Through valleys of shadows, we seek the light.
The chains that once bound us, now fall away,
In the reclamation, we find our way.

Whispers of wisdom, the ancients proclaim,
In struggles of spirit, lies grace without name.
Each tear that is shed, a cleansing of soul,
From ashes we rise, and we become whole.

With open hands lifted, we seek to embrace,
The power of love, in this sacred space.
Threads of redemption, stitch through the whole,
In the journey of healing, we reclaim the soul.

Together in prayer, we gather as one,
United in purpose, till the victory's won.
In hearts intertwined, we rise from the fall,
For the reclamation, vital to all.

Manifesting Grace amid the Grave

In the stillness of twilight, where shadows reside,
Hope flickers softly, our faithful guide.
Among the remains, where silence will reign,
We manifest grace to break through the pain.

With every lost moment, a seed must be sown,
In the soil of the heart, true love has grown.
Among the cold stones, a warmth appears,
The spirit of grace wipes away all fears.

Emerging like flowers from cracks in the earth,
We celebrate life and the miracle of birth.
With hands raised to heaven, we gather the light,
Transforming the dark into beautiful sight.

Through valleys of echoes, sweet melodies soar,
Resurrecting joy that was lost long before.
With faith as our armor, unbroken we stand,
Manifesting grace, with love close at hand.

Together we find, in this cycle divine,
Amidst the grave's shadows, our spirits align.
In remembrance and peace, our hearts softly wave,
For grace is alive, even here in the grave.

Remnants of Light in the Dark

In the depth of the night, where shadows creep,
A flicker of hope begins to seep.
Remnants of light, like stars in the black,
Guide weary hearts on their luminous track.

Though darkness may cloak us, our spirits ignite,
With whispers of love, to pierce through the night.
Each glimmer a promise, a beacon of grace,
In the fabric of faith, we find our place.

With tender compassion, we gather as one,
In the height of our struggle, we rise with the sun.
Remnants of peace, like dew on the grass,
Nourish our souls, as the shadows pass.

Through trials and storms, we face our fate,
In the arms of each other, we carry our weight.
The remnants of light, not easily seen,
In the dark, they shimmer, a hope evergreen.

With hearts intertwined, we journey ahead,
In the embrace of love, our spirits are fed.
Each moment a blessing, as we play our part,
Finding remnants of light in this darkness of heart.

From Grief to Glory

In shadows deep, we learn to pray,
With every tear that finds its way.
From sorrow's grip, we rise anew,
To find the dawn, the grace we pursue.

Through valleys low, our spirits strain,
Yet faith remains, a balm for pain.
We gather strength from those we've lost,
Their memories guide, no matter the cost.

In darkest nights, a flicker glows,
A promise made, as love bestows.
With heavy hearts, we lift our song,
From grief to glory, we shall belong.

Through trials fierce, and storms we face,
We find the light, a warm embrace.
In unity, our voices blend,
From sorrow's end, our hearts transcend.

So let us walk this sacred road,
With every step, our burdens unloaded.
For in the end, we find our way,
From grief to glory, come what may.

The Light that Weaves Us Whole

In whispers soft, the Spirit calls,
A thread of light, that never falls.
Each soul we touch, a part we share,
Together woven, in sacred care.

From heart to heart, the love flows bright,
Illuminating the darkest night.
In every prayer, a hope we sow,
The light that weaves us, it starts to grow.

Along this path of sacred trust,
We find our truth, our sacred dust.
In every moment, we see the grace,
That binds us all in this holy space.

Through trials faced, through joys embraced,
The light of love cannot be replaced.
With open hands and spirits whole,
We lift each other, united soul.

So let us shine, in joy and pain,
For in the light, we'll never wane.
Together, we stand and break the mold,
The light that weaves us, forever bold.

Revelations in Remnants

In broken pieces, beauty hides,
Each shard a story, where grace abides.
In remnants left of dreams long past,
We find the strength to ever last.

With every scar, a lesson learned,
In trials faced, our spirits burned.
From ashes rise, a phoenix flight,
Revelations found in darkest night.

In whispered truths, we recognize,
The golden threads that tie the skies.
Through fractured paths, our hearts unite,
In remnants cherished, we find our light.

So gather close, beloved friends,
In every ending, a beauty mends.
For life unfolds in sacred rhyme,
Revelations bloom, transcending time.

In the tapestry of joy and strife,
We stitch our souls to share this life.
In every moment, hold on tight,
Revelations whisper, we are the light.

Embracing the Unseen Grace

In quiet moments, we find our peace,
A still small voice, our soul's release.
Through silent prayers and hearts that yearn,
Embracing grace, we start to learn.

In everyday life, the sacred glows,
In acts of kindness, our spirit grows.
With open hands, we share our love,
Embracing grace, a gift from above.

Through trials faced and burdens shared,
We rise together, souls laid bare.
For in the struggle, we see the face,
Of unseen grace, a warm embrace.

So let us walk with faith unfurled,
Embracing love, a changing world.
In unity, we rise and sing,
For unseen grace, our souls take wing.

In every life, a story weaves,
Through unseen ties, the heart believes.
Embracing grace, we shine so bright,
Together, we are the sacred light.

Seraphim in the Fragments

In the shards of light, whispers sing,
Seraphim soar on angelic wing.
Each fragment glows, a story untold,
Gathering dreams, in hands of gold.

From the ashes, creation will rise,
In the depths of sorrow, beauty lies.
Heavenly hosts rejoice in the night,
Weaving the dark into threads of light.

Beneath the weight of a shattered sky,
Their voices echo, a lullaby.
Guided by love, pure and divine,
In every heart, their presence shines.

So let the broken find their peace,
In the embrace of grace that won't cease.
Each piece a part of the sacred whole,
Together, they whisper, merging the soul.

Seraphim watch, their vigil remains,
Through trials and tests, their light sustains.
In the fragments, the glory is seen,
A symphony played in the spaces between.

Healing Beneath the Celestial Veil

In twilight's embrace, we seek the balm,
Healing waters flow, soothing and calm.
Beneath the veil of stars that gleam,
Mirrored in hope, we find our dream.

With every tear, the heavens weep,
Love's tender hands our burdens keep.
In silence thick, the whispers fall,
Echoing grace, a gentle call.

Wounds may ache, yet spirits rise,
Transcending pain, we touch the skies.
In every trial, a lesson learned,
With faith, the weary heart is turned.

Among the clouds, the angels tread,
Bringing light where shadows spread.
With each dawn, new gifts are given,
Healing is found, and souls are risen.

So let us walk, with hearts aflame,
In love's embrace, we rise and claim.
Beneath the veil, we'll always find,
The touch of heaven, sweet and kind.

The Light within the Broken

In the fractures of life, light breaks in,
Illuminating the shadows within.
Each wound a path to greater grace,
A testament of love's warm embrace.

From the depths of sorrow, hope appears,
Dancing softly, dissolving fears.
Within the shards, a brilliance glows,
In the silent prayer, the spirit grows.

With every struggle, we learn to see,
The beauty in scars, the soul set free.
In the heart's turmoil, wisdom stirs,
A melody echoed in gentle purrs.

The light is found in broken things,
In the nature of love, the healing springs.
What once was lost can be regained,
In the tapestry of love, uncontained.

So cherish the light that dwells inside,
For in every fracture, love will abide.
Our journeys weave through pain and strife,
To reveal the light that gives us life.

A Pilgrimage through the Debris

Through the ruins, we make our way,
A pilgrimage where shadows play.
With every step, the ground we tread,
Holds the stories of those who've led.

Amidst the debris, the heart is stirred,
In the silence, a voice is heard.
The echoes of faith ring clear and strong,
Guiding our feet, where we belong.

In the rubble, seeds of hope are sown,
From broken paths, the light is grown.
Each stone a prayer, each thorn a plea,
In the journey's depth, we find the key.

With open hearts, we gather the past,
Finding the beauty that's meant to last.
In every sorrow, a lesson found,
In love's vast ocean, forever bound.

So let us wander through what remains,
Transforming loss into sacred gains.
For in the debris, a vision new,
A pilgrimage of life's enduring hue.

Covenant of the Reawakened

In shadows deep, the light was born,
A whisper soft, a spirit sworn.
From ashes rise, the heart takes flight,
Embracing grace, dispelling night.

In faith we stand, our hands held high,
With every prayer, we touch the sky.
The promise made through love so pure,
A sacred bond, our hearts endure.

Through trials faced, we find our strength,
In unity, we go the length.
With open eyes, we see the way,
The dawn will break, a brand new day.

The journey long, yet we're not alone,
In every step, His love is shown.
The covenant forged in fire and tears,
A testament to all our years.

We walk as one, with purpose clear,
In harmony, we cast out fear.
Each soul a spark, divine and bright,
Together bound, we seek the light.

Divine Alchemy of the Heart

From leaden weight to golden gleam,
The heart transforms, a sacred dream.
In stillness found, we find our voice,
In reverence, we make the choice.

Through trials deep, our spirits rise,
In darkest night, we seek the skies.
The essence pure, we melt and mold,
In love's embrace, our stories told.

Each tear a drop, a potion rare,
With every breath, we're woven fair.
Transcending self, we blaze the trail,
In unity, we shall prevail.

In sacred dance, the heart does sing,
With every beat, our praises ring.
The alchemy of love Divine,
Transforms the soul, and we entwine.

With every bond, a golden thread,
In harmony, our paths we tread.
Through faith we rise, our spirits soar,
In this divine, we are restored.

The Resurrection of Dreams

From ashes cold, new visions bloom,
In whispered hope, dispelling gloom.
The spirit stirs, a sacred flight,
In darkness found, we chase the light.

With every tear, a seed is sown,
In fertile ground, the heart has grown.
Awakened whispers, sweet and clear,
The dreams return, we have no fear.

In fractured paths, the way is steep,
Yet in our hearts, the promises keep.
Each step we take, a dance of grace,
The resurrection, our true embrace.

Together bound, we raise the flame,
In unity, we call His name.
With faith renewed, we rise again,
In love's embrace, we shall ascend.

The canvas waits, for colors bright,
Painting lives in purest light.
Forged by trials, strong and steep,
In every dream, our souls shall leap.

Chronicles of the Redeemed

In ancient scrolls, our stories lie,
The paths we've walked, the battles nigh.
With every word, a truth unfolds,
The tale of hearts, both brave and bold.

From depths of pain to heights of grace,
In every trial, we find our place.
The peace despite, the storms we face,
In love's embrace, we find our space.

The pages turn, the ink runs deep,
With every tear, our souls do leap.
In unity, our voices blend,
The chronicles of those who mend.

Through faith restored, we write anew,
With hearts ablaze, we shall pursue.
Each chapter weaves a golden thread,
In hope and love, the pain is shed.

In timeless tales, we see the light,
In every heart, a guiding sight.
The chronicles of grace divine,
In love, we stand, forever shine.

The Spirit's Return to Eden

In shadows deep where silence breathes,
A whisper calls through twilight leaves.
The path of grace, with light adorned,
Calls forth the soul to be reborn.

Beyond the gate, a garden blooms,
In every heart, the spirit looms.
With every step, redemption sings,
Restoring hope, as new life springs.

The rivers flow with sacred haste,
Nurturing the earth embraced.
Where angels tread and blossoms play,
The spirit's joy shall light the way.

In Adam's path and Eve's sweet glance,
The dance of love, a holy chance.
In every heartbeat, dreams ignite,
To live in truth, to walk in light.

So let us wander, hand in hand,
In Eden's grace, we'll make a stand.
Each breath a prayer, each moment sweet,
In spirit's peace, our lives complete.

From Sorrow to Sanctuary

In valleys low, where shadows creep,
A heart once lost begins to weep.
Yet in this pain, a voice ascends,
A promise held, where hope transcends.

The storm may rage, the night may fall,
But faith will rise above it all.
In solemn whispers, grace will flow,
Transforming tears to gentle glow.

The sanctuary waits for those,
Who seek the light that gently grows.
Through brokenness, the spirit mends,
Each sorrow shared, salvation lends.

With every prayer a light unfolds,
In quiet hearts, the truth enfolds.
From ashes rise, a vibrant hymn,
To find the love that lives within.

So let us journey, hand in hand,
From sorrow's depths to promised land.
In every trial, a glimpse of grace,
In sanctuary, we find our place.

The Choir of the Lovelorn

In hidden glades where longing sighs,
The heartache swells, the spirit cries.
Yet in the night, a chorus sings,
Of love lost deep and fragile things.

With every note, a story pours,
Of distant moons and open shores.
Each voice a thread in woven dreams,
A tapestry of silent screams.

Forsaken vows on whispered breeze,
Yet still the heart believes and flees.
In every tear, a memory glows,
A sweet refrain where love still grows.

The choir swells in dark lament,
With longing notes that heaven sent.
Each echo calls the soul to rise,
To find the light in love's disguise.

So let us join in sacred song,
In every love that's lost, or wrong.
For in the choir, we learn to cope,
From every heartache springs forth hope.

Forgiveness in the Emptiness

In empty spaces where shadows dwell,
The heart's forgiveness breaks the shell.
Each wound a crack, a path to light,
In silence deep, find solace bright.

For every grudge, a weight to bear,
Yet in release, we find our prayer.
With open hands, we let it go,
In the sweet soil, our spirits grow.

The emptiness, a sacred place,
Where love transcends and finds its grace.
In every scar, a story finds,
The hope that heals, the love that binds.

Forgiveness blooms in gentle tears,
Transforming pain into the years.
With every breath, a chance to mend,
In emptiness, we find the friend.

So let us walk with hearts so wide,
In every loss, love's arms provide.
Through every struggle, let us see,
Forgiveness brings us to the free.

Awakening from Ashes

From depths so dark, the spirit cries,
In silence, faith begins to rise.
Renewed in purpose, hearts ignite,
In ashes warm, we find the light.

The embers glow, a sacred spark,
Each whispered prayer, a vital mark.
Through trials faced, our souls refine,
Awakening grace, divinely entwined.

In storms of doubt, our courage grows,
With every step, our spirit flows.
From shattered dreams, we learn to fly,
Embracing hope, we reach the sky.

The journey long, yet worth the price,
Through pain and loss, we pay the slice.
With every tear, a seed we sow,
In fertile soil, our faith will grow.

In shared communion, hearts unite,
With love's embrace, we find our might.
Awakening from what has been,
To rise anew, with strength within.

Faith's Resurgence in Barren Lands

In barren lands where shadows dwell,
A whisper stirs, a sacred bell.
Through cracked earth, a promise gleams,
Faith blooms forth from ancient dreams.

With footsteps light, we tread the way,
In solitude, we learn to pray.
The arid winds may howl and moan,
Yet in our hearts, love seeds are sown.

Each struggle forged, a sacred rite,
In darkest hours, we seek the light.
From barren dust, our spirits rise,
As faith ignites the endless skies.

The way seems long, the night feels cold,
Yet warmth within begins to unfold.
With every breath, we share the fight,
For faith's resurgence shines so bright.

So let us gather, hand in hand,
In unity, we take a stand.
From barren lands, a garden's grace,
With faith restored, we find our place.

From Shadows to Sanctuaries

In shadowed valleys, we dwell near,
The echoes call, a voice so clear.
From desolation's dark embrace,
We journey forth to seek His grace.

Each trial faced, a lesson learned,
In life's crucible, the heart's discerned.
From broken roads to sacred ground,
In every loss, new hope is found.

Our spirits soar from depths we know,
Transformed by love, through pain we grow.
With faith as guide, we navigate,
From shadows deep, to heaven's gate.

In every tear, a prayer takes flight,
Uniting souls in endless light.
From darkened paths, our hearts align,
Creating sanctuaries divine.

Together strong, we rise anew,
In every moment, the sacred view.
From shadows bleak to places blessed,
In faith we find our hearts at rest.

The Dawn After Despair

When night has fallen deep and long,
A distant whisper sings a song.
Through darkest times, we find our way,
For hope reborn brings forth the day.

In trials faced, our spirits bend,
Yet faith persists, a faithful friend.
The dawn will break, with colors bright,
Chasing away the clouds of night.

Each tear we shed, a story told,
Of battles fought and hearts made bold.
For every heart that beats in prayer,
Awaits the light, a love laid bare.

The sun will rise, our fears will fall,
In every heart, a sacred call.
For after despair, joy will burst,
In gratitude, we quench our thirst.

So let us gather, hand in hand,
And face the dawn, together stand.
With hope restored, and love's embrace,
The dawn awaits, a perfect grace.

The Celestial Cloak of Courage

In shadows deep, where doubts arise,
A cloak descends from heavenly skies.
With threads of strength, woven with care,
It shields our hearts from worldly despair.

In moments fierce, when spirits wane,
This celestial gift breaks every chain.
With courage fierce, we stand tall and true,
Guided by the light that shines anew.

The call to rise from fear's embrace,
We wear this cloak; it grants us grace.
Emboldened souls, we forge our way,
With courage bright, come what may.

Through trials faced and battles fought,
In every tear, a lesson taught.
The cloak of courage, stitched with love,
A testament to the strength above.

So let us walk, hand in hand,
In faith and hope, a steadfast band.
Together bound by truth's own thread,
We don the cloak, our spirits fed.

Divine Reconstruction

In time's embrace, we break and mend,
Through trials faced, our souls ascend.
With hands divine, the Creator's might,
Rebuilds the heart, ignites the light.

From shattered dreams, the pieces fall,
Yet in the ashes, we hear the call.
A blueprint forged in love's design,
Our spirits rise, a sacred sign.

Constructed strong on faith's foundation,
We find our path, a true revelation.
Each fracture healed with gentle grace,
The Son of Light, our warm embrace.

In trials faced, divinely spun,
The threads of life, when joined as one.
We trust the hands that shape and mold,
In sacred stories, our lives unfold.

Through every storm and raging sea,
We are rebuilt in harmony.
With faith anew, our spirits soar,
Divine reconstruction, forevermore.

Awakening the Heart of the Hollow

In silence deep, where echoes dwell,
A hollow heart, a whispered spell.
Awake, arise, from slumber's grip,
For love's embrace, we yearn and sip.

The gentle call of hope so near,
A voice that quells our deepest fear.
Awakening dreams long laid to rest,
In faith we find, the heart's true quest.

With every breath, the spirit stirs,
Through prayer's embrace, the essence purrs.
Transforming darkness into light,
A journey taken, pure and bright.

In sacred moments, time suspends,
The hollow heart begins to mend.
With love's sweet touch, the spirit flows,
Awakening grace, the heart bestows.

So let us stand, united strong,
In every breath, we sing our song.
Awake, arise, for we are whole,
Awakening the heart, the essence, the soul.

Faith's Fabric in Faded Places

In faded places, where hope feels lost,
Faith's fabric weaves despite the cost.
Each thread a prayer, each stitch a dream,
A tapestry bright, a radiant beam.

Through trials faced and shadows cast,
We gather strength from the echoes past.
In gentle hands, the fabric holds,
The stories rich, the love unfolds.

When tears may stain the woven seam,
In every heart, we find the dream.
For faith endures, like morning light,
In faded spaces, it shines so bright.

A quilt of memories, stitched with care,
Embracing all, the weight we bear.
With every fold, a lesson learned,
In faith's embrace, our spirits burned.

So stand with me in faded grace,
We'll weave our truths, in every place.
For faith's fabric is never torn,
In love's great journey, we are reborn.

Soul's Sanctuary amid Scars

In the silence of the heart's deep night,
Lies a refuge bathed in soft, pure light.
Where echoes of pain find a gentle release,
And weary spirits can finally cease.

Here love's embrace mends what was torn,
In sacred whispers, the spirit is reborn.
Each scar a story, etched on the soul,
In this sanctuary, we become whole.

With faith as our guide, we walk through the fire,
Transforming our trials to heavenly choir.
Where tears may fall, they become streams of grace,
In the sanctuary's arms, we find our place.

Let burdens be lifted, let sorrows depart,
In this holy haven, we open our heart.
For in every wound, there's a lesson divine,
In soul's sanctuary, our spirits entwine.

So gather your courage, lift up your eyes,
Through valleys of shadows, our faith will arise.
With every heartbeat, let love be our chart,
In the soul's sanctuary, we play our part.

The Invisible Sanctuary

Beyond the veil of the seen and the known,
Lies a refuge where seeds of hope are sown.
Invisible walls of grace and of peace,
In this sacred space, our fears find release.

With faith as a compass, we navigate plight,
In shadows and doubts, we turn towards the light.
An unseen blessing whispers through the air,
In the invisible sanctuary, we're held in prayer.

Each breath a reminder of love intertwined,
In silence we listen, our spirits aligned.
The world may be stormy, yet here we are strong,
In the sanctuary's warmth, we always belong.

Let us wander the paths of the heart's gentle grace,
Where joy and forgiveness find their embrace.
Though unseen by eyes, the spirit can feel,
In the invisible sanctuary, our wounds start to heal.

Together we gather, in spirit and soul,
With love as our banner, we reach for the whole.
An unbreakable bond, a light from within,
In the invisible sanctuary, our journey begins.

From Discord to Divine Harmony

From chaos to stillness, each note we explore,
In the echoes of discord, we seek to restore.
With hearts open wide, we learn to perceive,
The beauty in fractures that teach us to believe.

In the dance of existence, we weave and we sway,
Transforming our struggles in luminous play.
From anger to kindness, the journey is long,
Yet in every discord, we find our true song.

Let melodies cross where our spirits take flight,
In harmony's glow, we embrace the pure light.
Together we rise, our voices unite,
From discord to harmony, we shine ever bright.

In the tapestry woven of love and of grace,
We learn to forgive and to hold each embrace.
Embracing the journey, our hearts whisper truth,
From discord to harmony, we find our lost youth.

So gather, dear kin, as the world sings along,
In unity's rhythm, we dance to belong.
With faith in our hearts, let's sing from within,
From discord to harmony, together we win.

Clarity in the Chaos

Amidst the swirling storm, a calmness we seek,
In the heart of the chaos, our spirits won't weaken.
With eyes open wide, we embrace what we face,
Finding clarity's light in this turbulent place.

When winds howl and rage, let stillness be found,
In the depths of the struggle, our souls are unbound.
Each moment a chance to rise above strife,
In chaos we gather, discovering life.

Let faith be our anchor, our guide through the night,
In shadows of doubt, we can find the bright light.
With every breath taken, let worries give way,
To the clarity glowing in each passing day.

Amid the confusion, look deeper, be still,
In the heart of the storm, find the strength of your will.
For the chaos will fade, and we'll see what is true,
In clarity's embrace, our vision renews.

So step forth with courage, let your spirit soar,
In the clarity gained, let us fear not the roar.
With love as our beacon, we'll navigate lows,
Finding peace in the chaos, as wisdom bestows.

Sacred Renewal

In gardens where the angels tread,
Life blooms anew from the heart's thread.
Each raindrop sings a hymn of grace,
As whispers of love in the sacred space.

With every dawn, the spirit flies,
Awakening under the vast, bright skies.
Paths of light, our souls shall trace,
In unity, we find our place.

The past, a canvas of lessons learned,
In flames of passion, our spirits turned.
Forgiveness flows like a gentle stream,
In sacred renewal, we dare to dream.

Seek the truth in the silent prayer,
Embrace the light, let go of despair.
From ashes of yesterday, we rise,
In the sacred embrace, our spirit flies.

With faith, we sow the seeds of hope,
In every heart, love learns to cope.
Together we stand, hand in hand,
In this sacred renewal, our souls expand.

The Altar of New Beginnings

Upon the altar, dreams ignite,
In the stillness, hearts take flight.
Casting off the weight of the past,
With each new breath, our shadows cast.

Promises whispered in sacred tones,
In vibrant colors, the spirit zones.
Through trials faced, strength does find,
The open arms of love, entwined.

Wounds of yesterday heal in time,
As the spirit rises, fresh as rhyme.
New beginnings beckon from above,
Wrapped in the warmth of endless love.

In the shadows, light prevails,
Guiding us where hope unveils.
On the altar, we lay our fears,
Offering all, through laughter and tears.

Each moment a chance to restart,
With humble whispers, we draw from the heart.
Together we build, side by side,
At the altar of new beginnings, we abide.

Transcendence Amidst Tribulation

In valleys deep, the spirit yearns,
For hope to shine, and wisdom learns.
When storms arise, and shadows fall,
We rise above, we hear the call.

For every trial, a lesson sown,
In struggle, we find strength we've known.
Like the phoenix, from ashes we soar,
Transcending pain, forevermore.

With faith unbroken, we walk the path,
Through darkness and doubt, we find our wrath.
With hearts aflame, we face the night,
In transcendence, we seek the light.

Every tear a river, leading to peace,
In the heart's embrace, all troubles cease.
Together we rise, hand in hand,
Through tribulation, we make our stand.

For in the trials, our spirits grow,
With each heartbeat, love's truth we know.
In transcendence, the soul takes flight,
Finding solace in the sacred light.

Ascending from the Abyss

From the depths where silence dwells,
We wander through life's hidden wells.
In shadows deep, we search for light,
Ascending from the abyss, we unite.

Echoes of hope in the stillness rise,
Guiding our hearts towards the skies.
Through sorrow's grip, we find our way,
In faith's embrace, we learn to sway.

Each step we take, a sacred climb,
Transcending limits, defying time.
With every breath, the spirit frees,
Ascending higher on whispered pleas.

In the abyss, we truly see,
The beauty of life's tapestry.
Together we rise, the dawn unfolds,
In unity, our essence holds.

From darkened paths to skies so blue,
We find our strength in love so true.
Ascending from the abyss, we shine,
In the divine dance, our souls align.

Celestial Restoration

In twilight's glow, the angels sing,
A promise made of hope shall spring.
From ashes rise, the spirit's flight,
To find the dawn, to seek the light.

Beneath the veil of starry skies,
We turn our hearts, we raise our eyes.
The heart does mend, the soul restored,
In grace enveloped, sweet accord.

From heavens high, the blessings flow,
Each tear transformed, a seed to grow.
Together we shall bridge the pain,
In faith we stand, our love remains.

The rivers cleanse our weary minds,
In sacred truth, our hope unwinds.
United under twilight's grace,
We seek redemption's warm embrace.

With every step on sacred ground,
A testament in silence found.
We journey forth, our spirits bound,
In celestial love, forever crowned.

Grace in the Grime

Amid the dirt, a spark of light,
In darkest hours, we find what's right.
Each shadow casts a fleeting trace,
Yet grace abounds in every place.

With open hearts, we seek to heal,
In life's rough edges, flaws reveal.
The weary find their strength anew,
In kindness shared, in love so true.

Through trials faced, we grow and learn,
In every storm, our spirits burn.
From broken clay, the potter makes,
A vessel bright, despite the aches.

The footprints left in sinking sand,
Evoke the touch of a guiding hand.
In grime we dwell, yet rise above,
With every breath, we share the love.

So let us dance in earthly mess,
Embrace the flaws, find happiness.
For in the grime, our spirits shine,
A testament to love divine.

From Wreckage to Worship

When wreckage falls, the heart breaks wide,
Yet through the cracks, the light shall bide.
In humble ruins, faith will spark,
A sacred flame that lights the dark.

The remnants speak of love once shared,
In whispered prayers, our souls are bared.
From shattered dreams, we rise anew,
With hands uplifted, hearts so true.

In silent screams, the spirit calls,
From brokenness, the newness falls.
We gather strength from stories told,
The warmth of faith, a hand to hold.

Through every trial, we chant our praise,
In life's wreckage, find holy ways.
A journey marked by scars and grace,
In worship true, we find our place.

Emerging strong, we lift our voice,
In ashes find a sacred choice.
For from the wreckage, we shall bloom,
In love's embrace, dispelling gloom.

Blossoms of Hope in Deserted Fields

In fields abandoned, hope will seed,
Where silence reigns, a gentle plead.
For in the dust, a promise stirs,
As petals bloom, the heart concurs.

Through parched and barren, life breaks free,
A testament of faith to see.
With colors bright against the gray,
Each blossom speaks of joy in sway.

The winds may howl, the storms may rage,
Yet still we turn each hopeful page.
From solitude, the spirit grows,
In quiet moments, love bestows.

With every bud, a whispered prayer,
Reminds us of the beauty rare.
In deserted lands, where shadows dwell,
The blossoms sing, a sacred swell.

So let us tend these fragile blooms,
With careful hearts, dispel the glooms.
For in each petal's soft embrace,
Lies promise bright, and boundless grace.

Fragments to Foundations

In quiet whispers, grace does flow,
Each shattered piece, a chance to grow.
From broken hearts, new hope will rise,
In faith's embrace, the spirit flies.

The light within can mend our soul,
With every fragment, we are whole.
Divine design in every crack,
Guiding us on our sacred track.

A tapestry of love is spun,
Binding all under the sun.
When darkness looms, the dawn will break,
Through every trial, new paths we'll make.

Together, we shall find our way,
In unity, we choose to stay.
The foundation firm, built on prayer,
In every heart, His love we share.

So let us walk with faith as guide,
Boundless love, our hearts must bide.
With every fragment, life rebuilt,
In sacred trust, our wounds are healed.

Covenant of Compassion Reclaimed

In solemn vows, our promise made,
To hold each other, not afraid.
With open hearts, we choose to see,
The grace in all, the unity.

Compassion's fire warms the cold,
A love renewed, a story told.
In hands held tight, we break the chains,
With every tear, our joy remains.

Together, we shall heal the land,
In kindness shared, we take a stand.
Each gentle act, a seed we sow,
From love like rivers, blessings flow.

No longer alone, we stand as one,
In shadows bright, we chase the sun.
With every voice, our song proclaimed,
The covenant of love reclaimed.

In faith, we will find our way,
Through trials faced, come what may.
An everlasting bond we forge,
With every heart, our spirits surge.

The Prayer of the Weathered

Beneath the storm, the weathered stand,
With weary hearts and open hands.
In trials fierce, our roots run deep,
Through every pain, our faith we'll keep.

Oh, weary souls, be not dismayed,
In darkest nights, His light won't fade.
A prayer for peace, our voices raise,
In humble gratitude, we praise.

Through crumbling walls and ancient stones,
A whisper speaks through weary tones.
In every wound, there's wisdom learned,
Each scar a gift, our spirits burned.

So let the winds of change blow free,
In every breath, His love we see.
The weathered hearts are forged in fire,
With strength anew, we rise, aspire.

United in our hope and fear,
In prayer, we find that He is near.
Through storms we face, we'll still believe,
For in His grace, we shall receive.

From Sorrow Springs Serenity

In shadows deep, the sorrow dwells,
Yet from the pain, a story tells.
Each tear we shed, a river flows,
In quiet grace, the spirit grows.

From aching hearts, a peace will bloom,
As petals soft, dispel the gloom.
In every struggle, love prevails,
Through darkest nights, His light unveils.

A gentle touch, the healing art,
Restoring faith, restoring heart.
With every dawn, the soul breathes free,
In sorrow's depth, serenity.

Embrace the journey, rise and stand,
With open hearts and steady hands.
For in the trials, blessings shine,
From sorrow deep, our spirits intertwine.

In unity, we share the load,
Together walking love's great road.
From sorrow springs, our hope's decree,
In every heart, your peace will be.

Awakening the Spirit

In stillness, the heart begins to soar,
A whispering breeze through heaven's door.
The sacred light ignites the night,
A spark of grace, a soul's true flight.

From shadows deep, the dawn does break,
With every breath, the spirit wakes.
In loving kinship, all is clear,
The divine presence drawing near.

Revealed in silence, the truth unfolds,
A story of hope, forever told.
In unity, we rise, we stand,
Guided by love, hand in hand.

The path of reverence, the way of peace,
In humbleness, our burdens cease.
Awakening grace, we find our role,
In every heartbeat, a sacred goal.

Embrace the light, let darkness fade,
In every prayer, the spirit laid.
A journey vast, through trials and tears,
We walk by faith, dismissing fears.

From Ashes to Glory

Out of the flame, a vision new,
From ashes bare, the hope shines through.
In trials faced, our spirits grow,
From darkest nights, the blossoms show.

With every stumble, lessons grace,
We rise again, to seek His face.
From brokenness, we learn to rise,
In faith's embrace, we touch the skies.

From despair's depths, our hearts are sewn,
To sacred ground, we have been shown.
With every tear, a seed is cast,
In joyous bloom, we leave the past.

In God's sweet mercy, we find our way,
In darkness dawns a bright array.
With open arms, we soar above,
From ashes deep, we shine with love.

In trust we stand, all fears erased,
With every struggle, glory graced.
Together bound, in truth we flow,
From ashes high, our spirits glow.

The Dawn of Resurrection

As morning breaks, the sun ascends,
A promise kept, where hope transcends.
With every ray, the shadows flee,
In every heart, a melody.

The stone rolled back, the burden lifts,
In emptiness, the spirit gifts.
From death to life, we rise anew,
With every breath, a vision true.

In joy we gather, hands entwined,
The faithful seek, the lost now find.
In unity, our voices soar,
To sing of grace forevermore.

The dawn of life, where love's bestowed,
Through trials faced, the truth erodes.
With every heartbeat, a sacred pledge,
In resurrection, we stand on edge.

With eyes uplifted, we see the plan,
In every soul, a holy span.
The dawn now breaks, the spirit thrives,
In love we walk, in hope our lives.

Transcending the Fall

In sacred whispers, the truth awakes,
Through every trial, the spirit shakes.
The burdens cast, like leaves in flight,
We rise anew, into the light.

From valleys low, we climb so high,
In grace and mercy, the soul will fly.
The chains of sorrow, we cast aside,
In divine love, we here abide.

With every breath, the dawning shines,
In endless love, where grace defines.
Through shadows cast, our path is bright,
In faith's embrace, we find our might.

The journey sacred, fraught with pain,
Yet in the loss, new life remains.
Through every tear, a lesson gained,
In every heart, love uncontained.

Transcending the fall, we rise above,
In harmony, we find our love.
In spirit's realm, forever free,
Together bound, in unity.

A Testament to Transformation

In darkness found, the soul does rise,
Emerging light, the spirit flies.
With faith as guide, the path is clear,
In trials faced, we shed our fear.

Each tear we weep, a lesson learned,
From ashes deep, a fire burned.
Through shattered dreams, new hopes ignite,
Embrace the dawn, a sacred light.

In humble hearts, the truth unfolds,
A tapestry of grace retold.
With every step, the heart does sing,
In the embrace of everything.

Rise up, ye weary, cast off your chains,
In unity, the love sustains.
For transformation is not the end,
But a journey shared, a means to mend.

In every struggle, find the spark,
A guiding flame within the dark.
Together we shall stand anew,
In faith and hope, the light breaks through.

Tokens of Triumph in Turmoil

In mountains high, where shadows loom,
Resilience blooms in desperate gloom.
Through valleys deep, our spirits soar,
With every challenge, we seek more.

Tokens of triumph, in pain we find,
A sacred bond, our hearts entwined.
With every trial, wisdom grows,
In storms of life, true strength bestows.

The echoes call of love's embrace,
In every struggle, a sacred space.
Together we rise, hand in hand,
In the tempest's eye, we take a stand.

Each victory gained, a testament clear,
In unity forged, we conquer fear.
As dawn breaks forth, the shadows fade,
In every heartbeat, hope is made.

More precious than gold, our faith shines bright,
In the darkest hour, we seek the light.
With courage ignited, our spirits sing,
In tokens of triumph, our hearts take wing.

Ethereal Echoes of Embrace

In sacred silence, the whispers flow,
Ethereal echoes, a love to bestow.
With open arms, the heart receives,
In gentle grace, the spirit believes.

The stars align in celestial dance,
Inviting souls to take a chance.
For in the night, the dreams take flight,
In ethereal echoes, we find our light.

Through winding paths, we walk as one,
Embracing truth 'til the work is done.
In every heartbeat, a song is sung,
In love's warm glow, we'll forever be young.

Beyond the clouds, where angels soar,
In radiant light, we ask for more.
The unity felt, a sacred bond,
In every breath, we wander fond.

Let every tear bring forth a bloom,
Transforming pain into sweet perfume.
In ethereal echoes, hearts entwine,
In love's embrace, our souls align.

Celestial Echoes Resounding

In the stillness, celestial voices sing,
Resounding joy as the heavens bring.
With every heartbeat, the truth released,
In sacred echoes, our souls find peace.

The cosmos whispers of love divine,
In every star, a promise entwined.
As moonlight graces the tranquil night,
In celestial echoes, we find our light.

Each moment cherished, a gift from above,
In trials faced, we're wrapped in love.
With open hearts, we share the light,
In celestial echoes, we stand upright.

From ashes rise, the flame within,
Transforming darkness into kin.
With faith as armor, we journey forth,
In celestial echoes, we embrace our worth.

In every prayer, a melody flows,
In harmony, the universe knows.
The echoes call, we heed the sound,
In celestial echoes, lost souls are found.

Fate's Favor in Fractured Times

In shadows deep where doubts do dwell,
Hope flickers bright, a sacred bell.
Guiding souls through trials grim,
With faith, we rise, our lights not dim.

Amidst the storms, a whisper calls,
Reminding us of grace that falls.
In fractured paths, we find our way,
With each new dawn, we choose to pray.

The road is long, but hearts unite,
In bonds of love, we seek the light.
Against despair, together we stand,
Fate's favor rests in gentle hands.

Let faith be our anchor, our song,
In broken times, we still belong.
With every trial, we learn to rise,
Embracing hope, we touch the skies.

So here we gather, hand in hand,
With whispered prayers, we make our stand.
In fate's embrace, our spirits shine,
Together weaving love divine.

A Hymn for the Hopeful

Raise your voice, let praises soar,
In every heart, hope opens the door.
With faith as our guide, we sing aloud,
A hymn of love, we lift our crowd.

In trials faced and valleys low,
With steadfast hearts, we choose to grow.
Each step we take, a sacred trust,
In hope we rise, in love we must.

The dawn will break, the shadows flee,
A promise kept, we shall be free.
With every tear, a seed is sown,
In gardens wild, our dreams have grown.

Join together, let your spirit shine,
In unity, our hearts align.
With every verse, a tale unfolds,
Of joyous hope, as life beholds.

So lift your voice and share the grace,
In every soul, let love embrace.
With hope alight, we find our way,
A hymn resounding, come what may.

The Testament of the Tenacious

From ashes rise, the tenacious bloom,
Strength forged in trials, dispelling gloom.
With courage as our steadfast shield,
In faith, our fate is gently healed.

For every tear, a lesson learned,
In the fires of life, our hearts have burned.
We stand as one, unbroken still,
With hope alive, we bend our will.

In battle fought, we claim our grace,
With every stumble, we find our place.
For in the dark, we light the way,
A testament of love each day.

Let voices rise, let spirits soar,
In times of doubt, we seek for more.
Together strong, we journey forth,
The tenacious heart, our greatest worth.

So here we vow, through storm and strife,
To cherish truth and honor life.
In every breath, a spirit bold,
The testament of souls retold.

The Spirit's Awakening Amidst the Ashes

In the stillness, a whisper blooms,
The spirit rising amidst the glooms.
From ashes cold, a warmth ignites,
With every hope, a vision lights.

In shadows cast, we search for grace,
With faith as our guide, we find our place.
Through trials faced, the heart takes flight,
Awakening souls to the sacred light.

With every breath, renewal flows,
In love built strong, the spirit grows.
In unity, we cast aside,
The doubts that once had tried to hide.

Let voices rise as dawn draws near,
Together strong, we banish fear.
In the heart's embrace, we find our truth,
The spirit's song, eternal youth.

So let us walk this sacred path,
With gratitude, we share the wrath.
In every moment, let love be shown,
Awakening spirits, we are not alone.

The Sanctuary within the Shattered

In cracks of despair, light softly gleams,
A refuge emerges, born from our dreams.
With fragments of faith, we weave our prayer,
A sanctuary formed from love and care.

Each tear that falls, a sacred release,
In brokenness, we find inner peace.
The heart reconnects, where shadows once lay,
God's whispers of hope guide our way.

Amongst the ruins, life starts to bloom,
In desolation, love finds its room.
Embracing the pain, we rise once more,
For in every heart, faith can restore.

Together we gather, hand in hand,
Building our strength upon this land.
Through trials faced, our souls become bold,
In unity's warmth, we break the cold.

The sanctuary thrives, where spirits unite,
In the shadows, we now seek the light.
Through whispers of grace, we'll always ascend,
In the sanctuary found, our souls will mend.

Seraphic Growth in Soul's Decay

From ashes of sorrow, the seed takes its flight,
In darkness, a promise ignites the night.
With wings of the spirit, we journey within,
Embracing the struggle, the battle begins.

In soil of despair, our roots intertwine,
A garden of grace, where the heart starts to shine.
Each moment of pain, a lesson imparted,
In seraphic embrace, we rise uncharted.

The shadows may linger, yet hope does remain,
Through turmoil and trials, we conquer the pain.
With every new dawn, a chance to renew,
In the depths of our soul, the light breaks through.

Birds of the spirit, we soar ever high,
On wings spun of love, we kiss the sky.
Through the storms of our life, we find our own way,
In the garden of faith, we choose to stay.

Seraphic growth blooms where spirits decay,
In the soil of sorrow, love finds its play.
With every embrace, the past gently fades,
And in this rebirth, our hope cascades.

The Reawakening of Faith's Flame

Amidst silent shadows, the embers lie still,
A flicker ignites, igniting our will.
From ashes of doubt, brave hearts shall arise,
In the reawakening, our spirit complies.

Through whispers of twilight, our prayers ascend,
To a realm where love and grace never end.
In soft gentle breezes, the flame starts to dance,
With courage and faith, we embrace the chance.

The soul's quiet yearning, a fire inside,
With each breath, we summon the strength to abide.
In devotion unyielding, we fan the bright light,
In the reawakening, our purpose ignites.

Together we travel, this journey of grace,
Through valleys of trials, we find our own place.
With faith as our guide, through the night we will roam,
In love's blazing warmth, we'll always find home.

The flame ever-growing, defying the night,
A beacon of hope, casting radiant light.
In the heart of the weary, our spirits proclaim,
The reawakening of faith's sacred flame.

Resurrection of the Spirit

In the depths of despair, where shadows reside,
A whisper of grace bids our spirits to stride.
Each moment of silence, a chance to be free,
In the resurrection, our hearts dance with glee.

From tombs we have built in the silence of night,
Emerges a promise, embracing the light.
With courage awakened, we rise from the past,
In the resurrection, our freedom holds fast.

The chains that once bound us, now crumble away,
A journey reborn, we'll follow the Way.
Through valleys of shadows, we carry our cross,
In faith's gentle hands, we embrace every loss.

The spirit once dormant now roars back to life,
Transcending the limits, transforming the strife.
With unity forged in the fires of love,
In resurrection's arms, we soar high above.

Together we flourish, our spirits entwine,
In the sacred dance, our souls brightly shine.
For in every heartbeat, the promise we feel,
In resurrection of spirit, our truth becomes real.

A Sanctuary of Hope

In a quiet place we find,
A refuge from the stormy night.
With open hearts and gentle minds,
We seek the warmth of sacred light.

The whispers of the spirit call,
They guide us through the darkest hour.
Together we shall never fall,
In faith, we bloom like hidden flower.

With every prayer, our souls arise,
Like birds that dance upon the breeze.
Beneath the watchful, tender skies,
We find the strength to bend with ease.

A sanctuary, this place we share,
Where hope abides and love will soar.
With every heartbeat, we shall dare,
To open wide our hearts' great door.

In unity, we bridge the gaps,
In peace, we gather hand in hand.
A place where kindness gently wraps,
Our spirits in this promised land.

Celestial Restoration

In shadows cast by earthly strife,
We search for light, for grace to shine.
The heavens offer hope for life,
A promise deep, a love divine.

Restore our hearts with gentle hands,
Let waters flow to cleanse our soul.
In nature's grasp, our spirit stands,
Renewed and whole, we feel the whole.

The stars above bear witness true,
To every tear and joyful cry.
In cosmic dance, we're born anew,
With faith, we touch the endless sky.

Let music play in vibrant chords,
As angels sing with voices clear.
We lift our hearts, in one accord,
To greet the dawn, release our fear.

Celestial grace shall light our way,
With every step, we shall embrace.
The love of God shall guide our stay,
In restoration, find our place.

Revived by the Divine Breath

With every sigh, we feel the dove,
A breath of life, so pure and rare.
The whispers sent from realms above,
Invite us to receive His care.

Awakened hearts rise from the dust,
In sacred moments, find our truth.
In stillness, we discover trust,
A bridge to wisdom, joy, and youth.

The Divine breathes hope into our veins,
Each heartbeat echoes His embrace.
We rise transformed, shedding our chains,
In gratitude, we find our grace.

Like morning mist upon the lake,
We sense the spirit drawing near.
As life unfolds, our fears awake,
But love dispels the dark with cheer.

Revived we stand, a flame anew,
In every trial, we shall proclaim.
United in His love, we grew,
In sacred connection, we reclaim.

The Garden of Renewal

Within the garden's gentle bloom,
   Hope rises like the morning sun.
Each petal whispers, casting gloom,
   Away, as light and life begun.

   We till the soil with tender care,
Our thoughts like seeds in earth we sow.
With faith and love, from pain we bare,
New life springs forth, a vibrant glow.

The fragrance of redemption sweet,
   Fills every corner, every heart.
   In unity, we join our feet,
   To dance as one, never apart.

As rain falls down, it nourishes,
The roots of dreams that dare to grow.
With gratitude, our spirit swishes,
   In trust, we let the river flow.

The garden thrives in joy and peace,
Each moment cherished, every friend.
   From every loss, we find release,
In love's embrace, our hearts ascend.

Embracing the Divine Echo

In whispers soft, the spirits call,
As shadows dance upon the wall.
In silence, hearts begin to yearn,
For light in darkness, a soul's return.

The nightingale sings a sacred tune,
Beneath the watchful gaze of the moon.
Each note, a prayer, a gentle breeze,
That carries love through ancient trees.

With every breath, the truth unfolds,
In every story, the past retold.
We find our strength in sacred grace,
In tender mercy, our rightful place.

Awake, arise, let spirits soar,
In unity, we seek the shore.
Together bound by faith's embrace,
A journey onward, a holy race.

The echo trembles, a heartbeat near,
In every doubt, hold love sincere.
Embrace the light, let shadows flee,
In harmony, we rise as free.

The Awakening from Darkness

From silence deep, a voice will rise,
In the stillness, truth defies.
Awareness grows, the soul ignites,
In dawning hours, the spirit fights.

Chains of sorrow break at dawn,
In gentle light, the fears are gone.
Emerging from the grasp of night,
We shed our doubts and seek the light.

Beneath the surface, the waters flow,
In every tear, the seeds we sow.
Transformation comes like summer rain,
Cleansing all through joy and pain.

With every step, the path is clear,
Let faith be bold, let hearts adhere.
In unity, the world will see,
The beauty found in you and me.

Awake, arise, O slumbering soul,
In love's embrace, we are made whole.
From darkness now, let hope ascend,
In every heart, the light we send.

A Celestial Symphony of Ashes

Among the stars, our dreams take flight,
In whispered songs that pierce the night.
Through ashes deep, the ember glows,
   In every heart, the spirit grows.

From fractured worlds, the beauty shines,
   In unity, the heart aligns.
The dance of dust, a sacred art,
Each breath a pulse, the end, a start.

In harmony, the echoes ring,
Each note a prayer that angels sing.
Clouds dissolve to reveal the sun,
In every heart, we are as one.

Celebration of the rise and fall,
In every challenge, we answer the call.
Ashes cradle the seeds of gold,
In every story, pure love told.

So hear the symphony of the skies,
In every note, the spirit flies.
A celestial dance, divine and true,
A melody crafted for me and you.

The Rebirth of the Believer

When shadows dim the fragile light,
Faith rises strong, igniting the night.
In sacred vows, our spirits blend,
A journey born, we start to mend.

Through trials fierce, we find our way,
In every sorrow, a chance to sway.
The heart, a vessel, full and wide,
In love's embrace, we shall abide.

Awakening dawn, the path appears,
In every heartbeat, a world endears.
Rekindled flames, the past now braves,
In unity, we rise from graves.

Through shadows cast, our souls align,
In truth's embrace, we redefine.
With every step, the light grows bright,
Rebirth of belief, eternal flight.

So rise again, O faithful heart,
In every ending, a new start.
As flames of hope consume the night,
The rebirth of dreams, a wondrous sight.

Milton Keynes UK
Ingram Content Group UK Ltd.
UKHW021913201124
451474UK00013B/723